3 Surefire Ways to Back Up Your WordPress Blog

By Ron Wilder
at KeepSmilingProducts.com

Contents

List of Figures

 By Ron Wilder

3 Surefire Ways to Back Up Your WordPress Blog

By Ron Wilder at KeepSmilingProducts.com
Copyright © 2010 WilderIP, LLC
First Edition: November 2010 – Rev 1.7

Notice of Rights

Notice of Liability

The author and publisher have made every effort to ensure the accuracy of the information herein. However, the information contained in this book is sold without warranty, either express or implied. Neither the author and Wilder IP LLC nor its dealers or distributors will be held liable for any damages to be caused either directly or indirectly by the instructions contained in this book, or by the software or hardware products described herein. By reading this document, you assume all risks associated with using the advice provided.

About the Author

Ron Wilder has been active in electronic and/or software design for over 40 years. Although he graduated in Electrical Engineering / Computer Science from U.C. Berkeley and is licensed as an Electrical Engineer, he has always considered himself a down-to-earth engineer who also enjoys working one-on-one with people to solve their technical problems. He loves to take napkin ideas and turn them into profitable tangible products. His favorite expression is: Keep Smiling! He can be contacted at www.KeepSmilingProducts.com/support

Introduction

It's 8:30am... What Happened to My Blog?

There you are... You're about to add a new entry to your amazingly popular WordPress blog.

But then...Oh Crap!

Your blog is gone, empty, nada!

It has vanished into thin air. All that's left is a single line:

> Ha ha -- Hacked By The WP Blog Zapper!

The reality hits you: Your blog is *Really Gone*!

Those agonizing words are staring at you where your once buzzing WordPress blog once was.

Do you panic?

Or do you laugh, confidently knowing that you'll be back up in less than 5 minutes... complete with all of the posts and comments.

Not many things strike more fear into bloggers than waking up to this scenario. Will you be prepared or will you throw your hands up in the air (*or worse*)?

The Choice Is Yours

Imagine the confidence you'll possess knowing you're in control; knowing that your WordPress Blog is backed up. And, knowing that you can quickly restore it to its working state: <u>Complete with all of the blog entries and comments.</u>

If you follow <u>just one</u> of the three step-by-step procedures detailed in this book, you will join the confident, laughing class of bloggers.

The choice is yours.

By Ron Wilder

STOP Blaming the Computer!

Third Time's a Charm

30+ years ago, I used to teach "office automation" to secretaries, engineers and managers of the US Air Force.

I used to tell people to backup their original documents.

I also used to tell them that they could blame the computer only the first time it happened.

The second time it happened, they only had themselves to blame.

Usually, there wasn't a third time. They had learned their painful lesson.

Well, that was 30 years ago, but not much has changed. Whether it's a floppy disk, CD, DVD, memory stick, hard disk, or network server, they ALL have to be backed up.

Another Nugget: If you lose your working copy, then you don't have a backup anymore. You only have a single document. So, try to backup your stuff to at least two different locations.

Don't delay. Save yourself from the pain. There's one thing for sure: Murphy lives inside EVERY computer and he's just waiting for the best time (*read worst time for you*) to attack and <u>laugh at YOU</u>!

This book will show you what you need to do so you can join the laughing (and confident) class of WordPress bloggers.

Overview of Three Methods to Backup WordPress

I will give you three step-by-step methods from easy to hard that you can use to backup your WordPress Blog.

1. **Paid Service**: The first is a pay as you go system where you pay someone else to do it for you. We'll give you a checklist of things you should ask the person backing up your WordPress blog.

2. **Low-Cost Purchased Utility**: The second approach costs a little money up-front, but simplifies the entire process so you can backup or restore your WordPress blog in seconds.

3. **Detailed Manual Steps**: This approach is totally free but requires more time, technical skills, and effort to master.

Each approach works and will accomplish the goal of backing up your WordPress Blog. The three approaches are contrasted in Table 1 in the areas of time and cost, and required technical skills.

Approach	Time	Cost	Tech Skills
Paid Service	----	Higher	None
Purchased Utility	Seconds	Low	Low
Manual	Hour+	Free	High

Table 1 - WordPress Backup Option Trade-Offs

All of the methods assume that you have installed WordPress onto a domain that YOU control.

*I need to mention that if you have created your WordPress Blog on WordPress.**com**, these techniques won't work!*

Besides, if you're serious about blogging, you'll want to host your own domain[1].

Again, the choice of how to backup WordPress is yours. In fact, you can use the free method described in this book right now for an emergency backup, to save money, o*r if you're just paranoid after reading the introduction.* ☺

Over time, however, you'll probably want to automate the process or at least make it less time consuming.

Whatever you, do. DO SOMETHING!

You'll only have yourself to blame if you lose your WordPress blog now that you know better!

---

[1] The least expensive approach is to buy a domain name from a web hosting company. You may get your domain name for free and the hosting runs about $5 to $7/mo. You'll also get free hosting of WordPress, email accounts, add-on domains (to allow you create lots of websites for no extra cost), shopping carts, unlimited storage, unlimited databases, etc. See the resources chapter for links to ones I use and recommend. If you'd like to view a webinar to see how to set this up, please let me know at:
http://KeepSmilingProducts.com/support
--Subject: Hosting Webinar Wanted

So How Do We Backup WordPress?

WordPress Consists of Three Pieces

Think of WordPress as consisting of three pieces:

1. Boilerplate stuff (virgin WP Install) which is installed each time you create a new WordPress website. This piece is the same for every site you create. Although the database is also created during the initial installation, it's basically empty... ready to be filled in as your blog is configured and posts and comments are added. Don't forget to write down your login information. You'll need this when you restore WordPress.

2. Admin Modifications, which change whenever you add new themes, plugins, widgets, or make other administrative changes that enhances your blog's appearance or functionality.

3. YOUR database, which is modified every time you add a post or comment, change anything in the admin area, including adding plugins and themes, etc.

It's relatively easy to backup the boilerplate stuff. The database stuff and admin modifications, on the other hand, require a bit more understanding of all things WordPress.

All three techniques described in this document will backup and restore both *YOUR database* as well as Admin Modifications.

The first and second methods will backup EVERYTHING, including themes, plugins, widgets, etc.

The backup *process* consists of two steps:

1. Backup your database

2. Save the backup somewhere safe

The restoral process requires the additional step of creating a virgin WordPress Blog and then restoring the previously made backup over it.

After you restore your WordPress Blog, it will be working again, exactly like it did the day (and moment) it was backed up.

     By Ron Wilder

Overview of the Three Backup Methods

As mentioned above, I'll start off giving you a list of questions that you should ask a friend or professional who will back up your blog for you.

Next, I'll let you know about an off-the-shelf product that you can buy and install that makes the back up and restoral process a snap. It is so good, that you'll be able to back up your entire blog in seconds. In addition, you'll also be able to restore it not only in your original location, but also to ANY domain that has WordPress installed.

Finally, I'll show you a step-by-step way to manually backup WordPress for free. Although you'll need some technical skills and a nerd's mindset, you'll be able to download freely available software and back up your WordPress blog without spending a dime... Well, except for the cost of this book. ☺

So, let's get started!

Method #1: Get Someone Else To Do It

So, maybe you have more money than time or don't want to blow up your brain trying to figure out how to back up WordPress, but KNOW you need to get it done.

Or, maybe it's not your "WOW" and you'd rather have a nerd take care of it for you.

No problems. There are people out there who LOVE doing this stuff. Remember those nerds in high school? Well, they've found their nirvana on the internet and live and breathe this stuff[2].

Where am I heading? Well, you can always pay someone to back up your blog for you.

If you decide on this approach, though, make sure to discuss the following items with the person doing it for you.

> Does the consultant <u>really know WordPress</u>? If they've only *used* it, then they won't know how to completely back it up (and restore) it.

---

[2] Wait, that's me! I have to confess that I'm one of them. I was one of those nerds in High School and still enjoy this stuff to this day!

 By Ron Wilder

Ask for references!!!

Discuss how often you want it backed up. This depends on your blog's activity. Does your blog change once a week, day, hour, or more often? As mentioned previously, the restoral point is the same as the last backup point!

Reliability of person or service: If this is your business, you'd better make sure that they will do the backups properly.

Make sure you get a copy of the backups. The last thing you want is if you DO need to have it restored and they're not available, you can give it to someone else to restore your blog.

What are their hours of operation? Will they be available 24/7 if your blog goes down?

Can you afford their fees?

Will you have a contract with them?

> Will you need a non-disclosure or non-compete agreement to protect your intellectual property rights?

In my opinion, the most important consideration is that you must be able to restore the backups being created for you.

Pick one of the backups they've done and restore it to a test location to make sure the entire blog is working properly.

This is YOUR responsibility.

If it doesn't restore properly, then you're out of luck. There's not much they can do to recover the data. Keep after them until you can get a successful restore to an alternate site.

Doing a test restoral periodically (once a week, or month, or so) will give you the peace of mind that you really can restore your WordPress Blog.

If you decide you want someone else to do your WordPress backups for you, please check out http://leapto.info/wpbackupsvc. It's certainly the easiest solution of the three in this book!

Method #2: Low-Cost & Simple WP Backup

Okay, maybe you want to save some money and are willing to do a little bit yourself.

Method #2 may be just the ticket. I'll now show you a really cool low-cost and easy-to-use WordPress Backup product on the market (wptbackup.com).

WordPress Backup for Non-Techies

Backing up WordPress doesn't have to be complicated, time consuming, or expensive.

Being a (*sometimes cheap*) techie, I tend to do things manually until the pain (*lost time*) is so great that I have to find something that will automate the task for me. Usually, my threshold is about $100 or so before I force myself to find a free alternative.

Luckily, I found the perfect solution at wptbackup.com.

This is a perfect example of a product that leverages someone else's expertise to handle a nagging pain such as backing up WordPress.

The fact that it costs so little makes it a no-brainer solution, in my humble opinion.

Oh yeah, not only can it backup and restore WordPress completely, but it also allows you to clone your blogs to as many sites as you wish!

All within seconds!

A Few Benefits

Here are some benefits:

- Backup your blog in seconds

- Restore your blog in seconds

- Complete database backup and restoral (plugins, themes, widgets, tags and categories, permalink structures and privacy settings, affiliate links, footers, headers, blog pages, posts, and comments, **Everything!**)

- Unlimited usage – Use as much as you like on all of the domains and WordPress blogs you manage.

- Works remotely from PC, Mac, iPad, iPhone, Android, etc.

 By Ron Wilder

- Clones ANY theme and ANY plugin set up This includes specialty themes like WishList (http://Leapto.info/wl) membership sites and Thesis Themes (http://Leapto.info/thesis)

- Create a WP sales letter in less than 7 minutes using the cloning feature.

- World Class Customer Support Hotline

- Very Low Cost

Just knowing that I can backup and restore WordPress in seconds is all I really needed, but when I looked at the other benefits, I was sold!

Simple Backup Steps

So, let's get started.

As you may recall, there are three phases required to back up WordPress:

1. Go to wptbackup.com to purchase and download, and install the utility. (*Do this once*)

2. Back up WordPress and save it to your computer. (*Once per backup*)

Phase 1 – Download and Installation

Step 1 – Get your own copy

The sales page at wptbackup.com has three videos showing you pretty much what I will describe below, but videos are better than text and pictures, so I'd *highly recommend* that you watch them. Even if you don't buy it, it may give you some other information you could use.

Note: Make sure to write down the email address you use when registering your product. You'll need to enter it when you restore your blogs later.

After purchase, you'll also get links to more videos that are updated as the software is enhanced. As of this writing, there are two videos: create-a-clone-1 and deploying-a-clone. Both are excellent and give you step-by-step instructions.

After downloading the product to your computer, make sure to unzip the file: **WP Twin-v??.?.zip**. (Substitute the version number that you've downloaded for the question marks.) Many Windows computers will unzip it if you just double-click on the zip filename. If yours doesn't unzip it, then download and install the free 7-zip (http://leapto.info/7zip) program.

Step 2 – Copy the Backup Utility to Your Server

Using an ftp program such as FileZilla (http://leapto.info/filezilla) ← Click.

Login and navigate to your server's WordPress blog page.

You should see the WordPress folders. (Fig. 1)

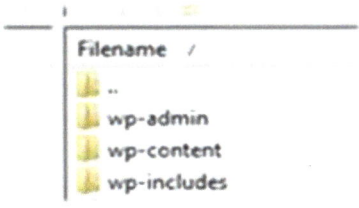

Fig. 1 -- WordPress Directory on Server

Next, on the left pane of FileZilla, navigate to the folder where you unzipped your download.

Now just drag the wptwin.php file from the left side into this directory on the right side. (Note: Don't drag it into a folder. Just drop it on top of a file to transfer it. (Fig. 2)

Fig. 2 -- Dragging the Utility to Your WordPress Server

In the above two steps, you've just transferred the script to your server so you can run it whenever you wish to create your backup.

Phase 2– Do the Backup and Download It

This is the phase that you'll do whenever you want to create the backup of your WordPress blog and save it to your computer. It shouldn't take more than a minute or two to setup and run.

Step 1 – Create the Backup

Run the backup script from your browser by going to your WordPress website directory. For example, if your WordPress blog is at myWPSite.com, then you'll enter myWPSite.com/wptwin.php into your browser (Fig. 3)

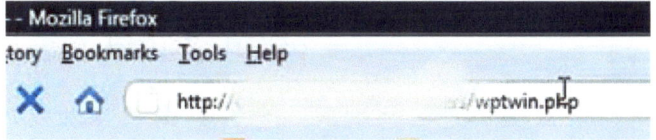

Fig. 3 -- Run the Script From Your Browser

Note: If you're not already logged in as the WordPress Administrator, you'll need to do so at this time (Fig. 4).

Fig. 4 -- WordPress Admin Login

After you start up the script, Click the button labeled "*Click to Clone this Site*" (Fig. 5) to create the backup of your WordPress Site! It will probably happen so fast that you won't think anything has happened!

Create Your Clone!

To create your clone, follow these instructions...

1. Choose Cloning Option

   ☐ Include Non-WordPress Folders

   Note: Selecting this option while cloning a blog on the Primary Domain will also include all Add-On domain files and folders in the clone, and will copy these to files and folders to the destination when deploying the clone. This is NOT recommended for a Primary Domain if you also have Add-On domains configured. If you are not sure what to do, leave this unchecked.

2. Click The Button Below

   Click to Clone

   [Click to Clone this Site]

   Click to Download

3. Download File to Your Computer Then Delete Clone
   Download: 2010-10-14 22:52:37   [Delete This Clone]

Fig. 5 -- Create the Backup (Clone Site)

Step 2 – Download the Backup to Your Computer

Download the backup file to your computer by clicking on the blue link: **Download: filename.** (Fig. 5)

When the download is complete, just click the "Delete This Clone" button to remove it from the server.

That's it! After you've done the above two steps a few times, it will probably take less than a minute to have a complete backup of your WordPress site.

Again, I highly recommend that you watch the videos on the wptbackup.com download site because they take you through the entire process that I've described here.

By now, you can probably see why I went with this approach. I can do a backup whenever I want in just a minute or two and it doesn't cost an arm and a leg to buy. This gives me the incentive to backup more often!

Restoring your Blog

In essence, the restoral process is to create a virgin copy of WordPress (just as you did when you first installed WordPress) and then update it with the backed up WordPress site you just created.

The following are the required steps:

Step1: Create a Virgin WordPress Installation

Please refer to the bonus chapter near the end of this book which will guide you through the process of creating a virgin WordPress blog website.

Step 2: Transfer Your Backup File and Restoral Script to Your WordPress Server

Once WordPress has been installed, start up your ftp program and transfer both the original site backup and **wptwindeploy.php** files to the new site's WordPress directory.

Use the same method as you did in Phase I Step 2 when you transferred **wptwin.php** during the backup phase, but instead copy the backup and **wptwindeploy.php** files to the server. (Fig. 6)

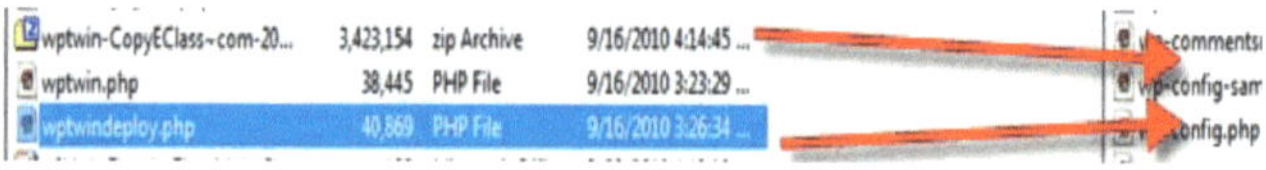

Fig. 6 -- Copy Both Files to Your WordPress Server

Step 3: Run the wptwindeploy.php on Your Browser

Now that both files are on your WordPress server, you'll need to restore the database to completely restore or clone your WordPress site.

Point your browser to your WordPress site's and add "/wptwindeploy.php" to the end of the URL address line. This will run the **wptwindeploy.php** script. (Fig. 7)

Fig. 7 -- Restoring Your WordPress Blog

Step 4: Validate Your Script

Since this is a purchased product, you'll need to enter the email address you used when you registered your purchase. (Fig. 8)

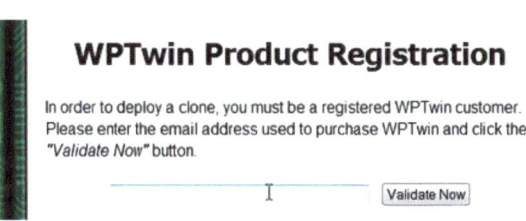

Fig. 8 -- Enter Your Registration email Address

Step 5: Restore your Blog (or Deploy the Clone)

After you've entered your registration email, all that's left is to restore your backup.

Click the *Deploy Clone* button to start that process. (Fig. 9)

Deploy Your Clone!

To deploy your clone, follow these instructions...

1. Choose the Automatic Clean-Up Options

   ☑ Delete Clone File After Deploying (Recommended)
   ☑ Delete WPTwin Script After Deploying (Recommended)

2. Choose the Clone File to Deploy

   CopyEClass.com (2010-09-16 16:14:28) ▾

3. Click the Button Below to Deploy the Clone

   [Deploy Clone]

Fig. 9 -- Restoring Your WordPress Site

When the green progress bar is done (Fig. 10), your original WordPress blog should be fully functional. Check it out!

n-CopyEClass~com-2010-09-16-161428.zip
):10 left   [63.1%]   2,162,688 bytes (120.1 KB/s)

Fig. 10 -- Cloning (or Restoring) the Backup

That's it! You've restored your WordPress blog.

If you end up using this method to backup, restore, and cloning YOUR WordPress websites, then you'll be eligible for some pretty cool bonuses. Check out the sales page for details: http://wptbackup.com/

Method #3: Free Manual WordPress Backup

The free method naturally will involve doing more "manual" work to backup your WordPress Database... but it IS FREE!

It isn't for the non-techie, though, so if you want to use this approach, make sure you have a techie friend nearby!

The method uses a freely downloadable public-domain php script called wp-db-backup.php.

Just as in method #2, there are two phases to this process.

1. Download and install the free plugin to your WordPress Website
2. Do the backup and save it on your computer.

The first phase is only done once because we have to get the plugin onto your WordPress web server.

The second phase is done each time you want to create a backup.

Phase 1 – Download and Install the Plugin

Step 1 – Download wp-db-backup.php

The first step is to copy the wp-db-backup.php file to your /wp-content/plugins/ folder in your WordPress directory on the server.

You can obtain this file by clicking the following link: http://leapto.info/wpbackup

Download this to your computer. (Just take note of where your computer puts the file.)

Step 2 – Unzip the wp-db-backup zip file

Right-click the downloaded file and unzip it.

If your computer doesn't recognize the zip file format, then you can unzip the file on your computer using a free program like 7-zip. You can click the following link to download the 7-zip program.

http://www.7-zip.org/

Just download the file and install it on your computer. I'm not going to go into details on this program since there's already plenty of good documentation available on 7-zip's website.

Step 3 – Extract wp-db-backup.php

After you've unzipped the wp-db-backup.zip file, examine the folder wp-db-backup. You should see something like Fig. 11.

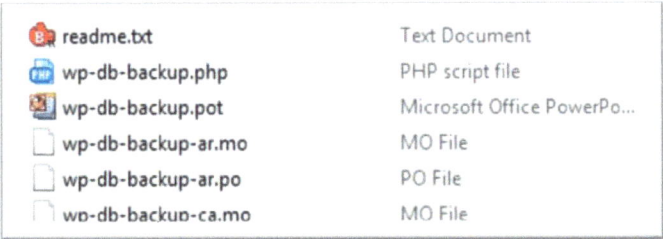

readme.txt	Text Document
wp-db-backup.php	PHP script file
wp-db-backup.pot	Microsoft Office PowerPo...
wp-db-backup-ar.mo	MO File
wp-db-backup-ar.po	PO File
wp-db-backup-ca.mo	MO File

Fig. 11 -- Downloaded wp-db-backup folder

There will be a bunch more files, but they are only needed if your language isn't English.

The only file we're interested in putting on the server is: *wp-db-backup.php*

So, go ahead and drag that file from the folder to your desktop or somewhere you can find it.

Step 4 – Transfer to Your Server

Now, you'll need to transfer the wp-db-backup.php script to your WordPress server's directory: **/wp-content/plugins/**

There are various ways to do this. I'd recommend that you transfer it using your favorite ftp program. A good free public domain one is FileZilla. ← Click

Since this book is focused on WordPress backup procedures, please review the documentation for FileZilla on the website or enlist the help of a friend who's familiar with uploading websites using ftp.

An alternate approach is to use cPanel which is standard on many linux-based hosted web servers3.

The bottom line is that you need to get the file into the /wp-content/plugins/ directory of your WordPress server.

---

[3] *If you would like me to write another book on how to use either file transfer approach, please let me know and I'll add that to my list of projects! The more people who request it, the higher it moves on my list! Please visit :*
http://KeepSmilingProducts.com/support

Please use the subject: **book request**.

Step 5 – Activate the plugin

Next, you'll need to activate the wp-db-backup plugin by going to your blog's Admin -> Plugins screen.

You can do this by first logging into your blog's Admin page. Usually, this is done by entering the following into your browser's address line.

http://*YourBlogWebsite.com*/wp-admin

You'll need to substitute your WordPress Blog's domain name for *YourBlogWebsite.com* above.

Then, click on **Plugins** on the left side of the WordPress Admin page.

Next, select "activate" on the WordPress Database Backup plugin of that page. (Fig. 12)

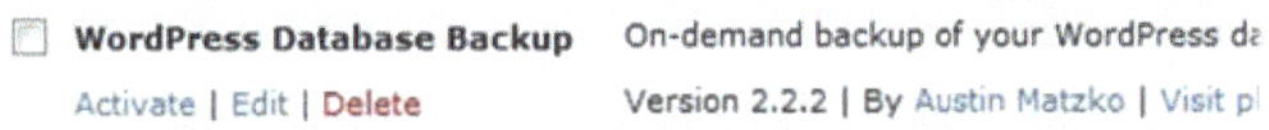

WordPress Database Backup   On-demand backup of your WordPress da

Activate | Edit | Delete   Version 2.2.2 | By Austin Matzko | Visit p

Fig. 12 -- WP DB Backup Plugin (before activation)

After you've done that, it should appear as in Fig. 13, below:

WordPress Database Backup   On-demand backup of you
Deactivate | Edit   Version 2.2.2 | By Austin

Fig. 13 – WP DB Backup Plugin (after activation)

The notes from the WP-DB-Backup Plugin website mention that you may need to make /wp-content writable (at least temporarily) to allow the installation to complete.

See the notes at: http://leapto.info/wpbackup

WHEW… The Hard Part is Done!

Remember, this only has to be done once per WordPress Site. The next piece is done for each backup.

Phase 2 – Make the Backup!

Okay, you've just installed the plugin. So now let's describe the backup phase.

There are two parts to this phase:

1. Backup the database

2. Backup the WordPress files

If you don't backup both, then you won't have a complete backup of your WordPress blog.

Part 1 – Backup the WordPress Database

Step 1 – Prepare to Backup WordPress

On the left side of the WordPress Admin page, click on **Tools** then **Backup** to get to the backup page. (Fig. 14)

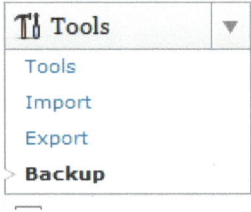

Fig. 14 -- How to Get to Backup Options

Just choose the default settings on the page except for the **Backup Options** choices.

Here's where you decide where you want your backup to go. I'd recommend that you copy it to your computer so there's no chance that a hacker could delete it. You can always upload it during the restoral process. (See Fig. 15)

I'd also consider using the "schedule" option so you can have automatic backups. Although I didn't show it in Fig. 15, you can find it further down the page.

Finally, I'd strongly recommend setting up a free "WordPress blog backup only" gmail account and sending regular backups to it. It's up to you...

Fig. 15 -- WordPress Backup Options

Step 2 – Start the Backup

Now do the backup by clicking on the *Backup now* Button. (Fig. 15) While it's working you'll see the progress bar. When it's done, you'll have the opportunity to save it (from within your browser).

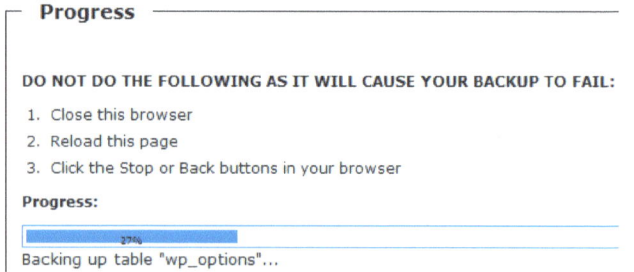

Fig. 16 -- Make Sure To Wait Until Done!

Step 3 – Save the Backup

After the backup is done, you'll end up with a file called something like:

xyz_wrdp3_wp_20101004_069.sql.gz

The piece labeled in red is the actual database name that you'll need to restore to later.

Save this file on your computer in a location that you'll be able to find later. This is the database restoral script that will be used during the restore process.

Part 2 – Backup the WordPress Files

Step 1 – Log into cPanel

Now, we need to backup the WordPress files and directories (which will also backup the themes, plugins, admin settings, etc.)

Note: Technically you only need to back up the files and the wpconfig directory, I always back up all of them. Call me conservative, but the additional time and storage space it takes is minimal.

You'll need to log into your website's cPanel. (*See Step 1 of the Bonus Chapter: Virgin WordPress Installation*)

Step 2 – Start up File Manager

Locate File Manager and select it to access the entire file structure of your website. (Fig. 17)

Fig. 17 -- Start up File Manager within cPanel

Step 2 – Compress Top-Level WordPress Directory

Navigate to your WordPress top level directory (Fig. 18)

Select All Files (Fig. 19)

Select "Compress" (Fig. 20)

Name the output zip file and then click the "Compress File(s)" button. (Fig. 21)

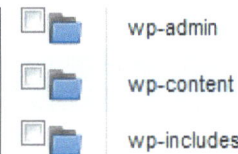

Fig. 18 -- WordPress Top-Level Directory

Fig. 19 -- Select All Files

Fig. 20 -- Select "Compress"

Fig. 21 -- Enter Output Zip Filename then Compress

Step 3 – Download the Compressed WP Directory

Locate the Zip file you just created (Fig. 22) and double click to download it to your computer into the same directory that you saved your WordPress database.

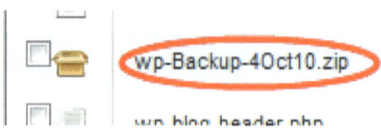

Fig. 22 -- Find the Zip File Just Created

You're done!

You've backed up your WordPress Website.

Like I said earlier, the free process is more work, *BUT IT IS FREE*!

If you're pulling out your hair after reading this, then maybe Method 2's low-cost *wptbackup.com* approach is for you. Although time isn't necessarily money, it does make sense to farm out stuff you don't like to do.

Manually Restoring Your WordPress Blog

Okay, you've backed up your WordPress Blog. Or have you? You won't really know until you try restoring it, will you?

In this section, we'll take the backup you made above and restore it to a test site to make sure it works.

The restoral process is basically to create a virgin copy of WordPress (just as you did when you first installed WordPress) and then update it with the backed up WordPress site you just created.

The following are the required steps:

Step1: Create a Virgin WordPress Installation

Please refer to the bonus chapter near the end of this book which will guide you through the process of creating a virgin WordPress blog website.

Step 2: Transfer Your Backup Database File to Your Server

Once WordPress has been installed, start up your ftp program and transfer the backup file that you created above (Step 3) to your server in the same folder as WordPress.

There is one thing to be aware of with regards to the WordPress database. In Phase 2, Step 3 above, you will find the name of the database in red text.

Make sure that the virgin installed database is the same name. If it isn't then make sure to install to that name, otherwise, you won't restore your blog properly.

1. Login to phpMyAdmin (Fig. 23)
2. Click databases, and select the database that you'll be importing your data into (Fig. 24)
3. You will then see either a list of tables already inside that database or a screen that says no tables exist. This depends on your setup.
4. Across the top of the screen will be a row of tabs. Click the Import tab. (Fig. 25)
5. On the next screen will be Location of Text file box and next that a button named Browse or Choose File. Click the button.(Fig. 26)
6. Locate the backup file stored on your computer.(Fig. 26)
7. Make sure the SQL ratio button is checked.(Fig. 27)
8. Click the GO button on the bottom right side of the page. (Fig. 28)

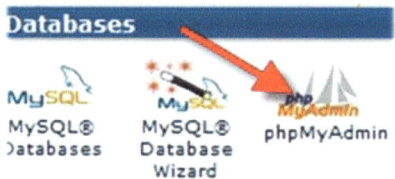

Fig. 23 -- log into phpMyAdmin in cPanel

Fig. 24 -- Select Databases

Fig. 25 -- Import the database

Fig. 26 -- Choosing the Database to Import

Fig. 27 -- Make sure SQL is selected

Fig. 28 -- Click the Go Button to Restore DBs

Step 3: Restore Your Backup WordPress Files

Now that the database has been restored, it's time to restore the WordPress Files and Directories to the server.

The process is the reverse of the File Backup procedure in Part 2.

Start the File Manager on the server and select the Upload button. Then find the zip file on your computer that holds the backed up WordPress files. Make sure you're locating the file inside of the top level WordPress directory

Next, select Extract from the bar at the top of the page. (Fig. 29)

Fig. 29 -- Extract Button

Be sure you're extracting the files to the correct location. Then click the Extract File(s) button. (Fig. 30)

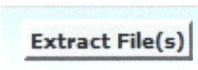

Fig. 30 -- Extract File(s) button

That's it! You should be able to log into your WordPress website.

Bonus: Virgin WordPress Installation

There are plenty of resources on the internet that can show you how to install WordPress on your host. These instructions are just here to tickle your memory in case you've completely forgotten how you did it the first time!

Step 1: Log into Your website's cPanel

Using your favorite browser, log into cPanel of your WordPress host. You'll need your website's login name and password.

A typical address to go to would be: http://myWPSite.com/cpanel. Replace myWPSite.com with your domain name. (Fig. 31)

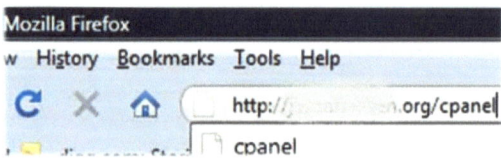

Fig. 31 -- Log into your Website's cPanel

Step 2: Install WordPress

Next, navigate with your mouse to Fantastico and select it. (Fig. 32)

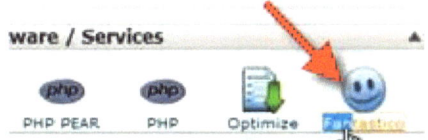

Fig. 32 -- Navigate to Fantastico

Install a New Copy of WordPress. (Fig. 33)

Fig. 33 -- Install WordPress

Fill in the WordPress blog data fields. Note that both the Site name and Description can be seen by the user. (Fig. 34)

Fig. 34 -- All is Cloned Except Site Name and Desc.

The result will be a virgin WordPress Installation. Note that the visibility of the Site Name and Description. (Fig. 35)

Fig. 35 -- Virgin WordPress (with Matching Site Name)

Go ahead and test out the blog. It should be a standard, unmodified WordPress blog.

At this point, you can either use it as-is, add plugins, themes, widgets, etc. or restore a previously saved database to get it back to where it was before.

If you want to restore a previously backed up database, please refer to methods 2 or 3, above.

Conclusion

Losing a blog CAN happen to <u>any</u> blogger. For some, it may not be that big of a deal, but for others, it can mean the loss of significant income and reputation and the cause of considerable frustration.

If your blog is hacked, your reputation could be damaged or worse: You may lose everything and have to start from scratch.

In this book, I've shown you how to completely backup and restore your WordPress blog. Three ways have been shown ranging from free to a couple of paid approaches.

The approach I've personally chosen and strongly recommend is to use a low-cost off-the-shelf product available at wptbackup.com to backup, restore and clone my WordPress sites. It's simple to install and even simpler to use.

The fact that you can clone a site in seconds opens up the possibilities of creating a "standard template" WordPress sales funnel with your favorite themes and plugins and then just cloning it whenever you want to create a new funnel for a new product you want to promote.

So, now it's your time for you to ACT! If you have a WordPress blog, then you REALLY should be backing it up.

Pick any of the methods and just do it.

You'll feel a lot better knowing you can quickly recover your blog.

Do it NOW before disaster strikes! Someone is probably trying to hack into your blog as you read this! It might even be Murphy, himself!

Resources

I invite you to visit this book's website:

http://leapto.info/wpbackupbookupdates

I'll also be doing a WordPress backup webinar where I demonstrate, step-by-step, both the free and WP Backup methods. After I demonstrate the methods, I'll answer questions from participants.

Keep smiling,

Ron

P.S. I've provided some links below to some useful products for you.

Free Utilities and Plugins:
FileZilla:

FileZilla is a free ftp (file transfer program) which can be used to copy files from your PC to your WordPress or any other Website.

http://leapto.info/filezilla

7-Zip:

If your computer doesn't recognize the zip file format, then you can unzip the file on your computer using a free program like 7-zip. Click the following link to the 7-zip download site:

www.7-zip.org/

WordPress Backup Products

wptbackup.com:

A low-cost commercial solution that backs up, restores, and clones WordPress blogs is available at wptbackup.com. It will copy EVERYTHING in the blog including all admin settings, themes, plugins, widgets, blog posts and comments, etc.

The more complicated your WordPress blog, the more you need a quick and reliable product to help out. It will even clone your purchased themes such as the WishList membership site theme to the sophisticated Thesis theme.

Oh yeah, it can be run from your iPhone, iPad or any remote web browser.

Bang! Done! Backed up! Cloned! Very cool!

Here's a link to the off-the-shelf utility:

`http://wptbackup.com` ← Sales Page

wp-db-backup:

This is the free WordPress backup plugin discussed in Method 1.

Don't forget that this ONLY backs up the WordPress Database, so you'll need to also backup the WordPress files and directory structure.

There is no equivalent restoral plug-in, though, so you'll have to manually restore everything.

You can obtain this plugin by clicking the following link:

`http://leapto.info/wpbackup`

Some Cool WordPress Themes

Thesis Theme:

Thesis Theme is a great all-encompassing WordPress Theme. Using your mouse in the Admin page, you can pretty much set up any type of WordPress appearance. Check it out!

`http://leapto.info/thesis`

WishList Theme

WishList is a great WordPress Membership site Plug-in. Lots of powerful features are just a click away if you're setting up a membership site using WordPress.

`http://leapto.info/wl`

Web Hosting / Domain Name Companies

Web hosting companies are everywhere. They all say that they're the best.

From my experience, it's the details that count as well as customer support.

I personally use two companies. One for my hosting and the other for the numerous domain names I've accumulated over the years.

I host with *LunarPages*. You get pretty much unlimited everything: storage space, bandwidth, add-on domains, databases, etc. Your first domain name is free as long as you host with them. The cost is about $5/mo. Sweet!

LunarPages: `http://leapto.info/lunar`

I also use *1and1* for some hosting, but primarily for low cost domain names that I point back to my Lunarpages websites.

1and1: `http://leapto.info/1and1`

Many others I've spoken to have had good luck with HostGator and HostMonster. Most of the benefits are similar to LunarPages.

HostGator:
`http://leapto.info/hostgator`

HostMonster:
`http://leapto.info/hostmonster`

www.ingramcontent.com/pod-product-compliance
Lightning Source LLC
Chambersburg PA
CBHW040853180526
45159CB00001B/413